if they didn't...
you wouldn't...

INDIA · SINGAPORE · MALAYSIA

if they didn't...
you wouldn't...

Christelle Faith Menon

INDIA • SINGAPORE • MALAYSIA

Copyright © Christelle Faith Menon 2024
All Rights Reserved.

ISBN 979-8-89519-842-1

This book has been published with all efforts taken to make the material error-free after the consent of the author. However, the author and the publisher do not assume and hereby disclaim any liability to any party for any loss, damage, or disruption caused by errors or omissions, whether such errors or omissions result from negligence, accident, or any other cause.

While every effort has been made to avoid any mistake or omission, this publication is being sold on the condition and understanding that neither the author nor the publishers or printers would be liable in any manner to any person by reason of any mistake or omission in this publication or for any action taken or omitted to be taken or advice rendered or accepted on the basis of this work. For any defect in printing or binding the publishers will be liable only to replace the defective copy by another copy of this work then available.

DEDICATION

To all the hearts that have been bruised and yearning,
For those who have felt the sting of unrequited love,
Who have longed for reciprocation in a world that feels one-sided,
This is for you.

To the ones who have questioned their worth,
Sought validation in the words and actions of others,
This is a reminder that your value is natural,
That you are deserving of a love that is true and fulfilling.

For every tear shed in solitude,
For every moment of doubt and loneliness,
Know that you are not alone in your experiences,
And that your heart is resilient.

May this book serve as a guiding light,
A source of comfort and understanding,
As you navigate the complexities of love,
And find solace in your own strength and self-love.

With deep empathy and unwavering compassion,
This book is dedicated to you,
In the hope that it will illuminate your path,
And inspire you to reclaim your worth and find fulfillment.

You are deserving of a love that is reciprocated,
A love that nurtures and cherishes your heart.
May you embrace your own power,
And rewrite the narrative of your life.

This dedication is a testament to your resilience,
And a reminder that you are worthy of a love that flourishes,
Free from the burden of justification and loneliness.

With heartfelt sincerity,
This book is dedicated to **YOU**.

PREFACE

In our journey through life, we often encounter relationships that profoundly impact us, even when they're not reciprocated in the way we hope. This book, **if they didn't... you wouldn't...**, is a reflection on those one-sided loves and the lasting emotional imprint they leave behind.

I wrote this book to address a topic that many of us experience but rarely discuss openly. The pain of unrequited love can be overwhelming, and navigating through these feelings can be challenging. Through this exploration, I hope to offer comfort, understanding, and practical insights for those who find themselves in the aftermath of such emotional experiences, in the same way I would have wished it existed for me.

The idea for this book came from my own personal experiences and the stories of others who have shared their struggles with me. These narratives, while deeply personal, highlight a common thread of resilience and growth. My hope is that by sharing these stories, readers will find solace and strength in their own journeys.

As you read through the chapters, you'll encounter various reflections and lessons derived from the complexities of one-sided love. Each chapter starts with the phrase "**if they didn't....**," setting the stage for an exploration of how such experiences shape who we are and how we move forward.

This book is not just about understanding the past; it's about embracing the present and moving towards a future where you can thrive, even in the wake of unfulfilled desires. I invite you to embark on this journey with me, with the hope that you find healing, clarity, and empowerment through these pages.

Thank you for joining me on this exploration.

With heartfelt sincerity,
Christelle Faith Menon

FOREWORD

In "if they didn't... you wouldn't...," the author bravely delves into her personal love life, unraveling a profound journey of self-discovery and transformation. Through a candid narrative, she shares experiences, each attached with invaluable lessons learned along the way.

This book not only documents the highs and lows of love but also serves as a beacon of hope for those navigating similar paths. As someone who journeyed alongside her, I can attest to its profound impact in times of darkness. It offers reassurance that despite the pain, healing is inevitable and growth is attainable.

For anyone seeking solace and wisdom amidst relationship challenges, "if they didn't... you wouldn't..." is a compelling read that promises to uplift and inspire.

– Syeda Fatima Zia Rizvi

In "if they didn't... you wouldn't...," this author meticulously unravels her struggles in the journey of self discovery in terms of love. Often taught how to love our other half or our close ones, people tend to loose the first step, being loving yourself.

The author not only wanted to pour out her thoughts onto paper but also create a path of hope for those struggling through the same tough lessons she navigates all by herself. I may have entered the narrative relatively later but watching her grow from what she was to what she is now is truly inspiring of how strong a person can be if they put their mind to it.

Healing is inevitable. A simple yet impactful lesson I learnt from her. For anyone seeking a hand amidst a challenging relationship, this book is your friend, the author is that person reaching out her hand telling you that you've got this and you'll get there soon!

– Jessica Antao

CONTENTS

Introduction	13
Chapter 1	17
If they didn't always gaslight you	
Chapter 2	25
If they didn't always doubt you	
Chapter 3	33
If they didn't pretend to love you	
Chapter 4	41
If they didn't make you wait	
Chapter 5	49
If they didn't claim you were a priority	
Chapter 6	59
If they didn't hide their feelings	
Chapter 7	69
If they didn't break promises	
Chapter 8	79
If they didn't feel like your forever person	
Chapter 9	87
If they didn't create the wounds	
Chapter 10	95
If they didn't love you	
Conclusion	105

INTRODUCTION

Have you ever fallen in love? The type of love where every text illuminates your life, where every phone call brings an electric excitement, and every moment together feels like a dream? It's a time when the world suddenly makes sense, and all the chaos of life fades away because two people have found a perfect union. This feeling of love, when purely and genuinely expressed, is a phenomenon that cannot be put into words.

But what if that love isn't reciprocated in the way you hoped? What if the intensity you feel isn't matched, turning every tender expectation into a source of heartache? Imagine the emotional struggle of finding yourself in moments when others fail to return your affection and embrace your happiness. Have you ever wondered how different you might be if those moments of unreturned affection were instead moments of mutual joy?

- What if they hadn't overlooked your affection?
- What if they hadn't dismissed your dreams as trivial?
- What if they hadn't decided to walk away just when you were ready to give it all?
- If they didn't leave, would you still be searching for closure?
- If they loved you back, wouldn't you have never known the strength that comes from heartbreak?

These are the questions that give this book its theme, "if they didn't... you wouldn't..." explores the issue of one-sided love and how feelings stemming from it keep people tied to what could have been. It's a journey through the highs and lows of young love, the kind that leaves a lasting imprint on our hearts and stays with us for the rest of our lives.

Why Read This Book?

This is more than just a simple tale of romance; it's a profound exploration of relationships and personal growth. It's about understanding that every heartbreak was sent to make you wiser and that each unrequited love was a gift because it made you learn more about yourself. This book dares you to consider how the course of your emotional journey might have been if matters of love turned out differently.

Through the stories of relatable characters and real-life scenarios, this book will take you on a journey of self-discovery and recovery. You will learn to handle those complex emotions that come with caring for someone who may not reciprocate your feelings in the same way.

Deepening the Exploration

Imagine the first time you realized your love wasn't being returned. Perhaps it was a simple, crushing moment when a smile wasn't mirrored, or a heartfelt message was left unanswered. These moments, small as they might seem, can carve deep wounds. You might remember the nights spent staring at the ceiling, questioning your worth and wondering what you did wrong. These experiences are universal, and this book aims to shed light on the beauty found in these dark times.

As you turn each page, you will explore instances where non-reciprocation led to a deeper understanding of self-love and resilience. Picture a character who pours their heart into a relationship, only to be met with indifference. Through their journey, you see the transformation that occurs when they finally let go and find solace within themselves. Their story becomes a mirror, reflecting your own experiences and offering a new perspective.

This book is dedicated to all who have experienced the joy of love and the pain of loss, and who strive to find happiness with a new partner. It is for the believers in the good found in isolation and the beauty in scars. The narratives within will guide you through the different stages of heartache and recovery, showing you that the harshest lessons often come with the greatest rewards.

Conclusion

Welcome to this enlightening journey through the different stages of heartache and recovery. Together, let's demystify how the things that others did to us, or the things we did to ourselves, made us who we are today. This is a story about recognizing the value of pauses and the strength of moving forward. It's about understanding that often, the harshest lessons are learned through challenges. This is your story, our story, about embracing the scars and finding the beauty within them.

1

IF THEY DIDN'T ALWAYS GASLIGHT YOU

1

IF THEY DIDN'T ALWAYS GASLIGHT YOU

Gaslighting—a term that originated from the 1944 film Gaslight, in which a husband manipulates his wife into doubting her sanity—has outshone its cinematic roots to become a stark reality for many. In the realm of love, gaslighting is particularly dangerous, distorting not only perceptions of love and trust but also the very perception of oneself.

The Subtle Beginnings

Imagine doubting your feelings, your memories, even your very reason for being, within a relationship where you should feel safe and secure. It starts innocently enough: a few negative remarks, a condescending glance, or a careless gesture that plants seeds of uncertainty. Over time, these seeds grow into a dense forest of confusion, where the light of your reality is overshadowed by detachment.

The Echoes of Doubt

The journey begins with small, almost undetectable moments. You recall a conversation one way, but your partner insists it happened differently, dismissing your concerns as overreactions. Phrases like, "You're imagining things," "You're too sensitive," or "It's just a joke," become common. Slowly, these instances pile up, each one chipping away at your confidence, leaving you questioning your sanity.

In my own experience, I remember the endless cycles of conflicts where I was constantly cast as the villain. Regardless of the circumstances, every dispute seemed to warp and twist until I was at fault. This pattern led me to doubt my reactions, thinking, "Maybe I am too sensitive." I began to believe that the chaos was my doing, that perhaps I was the problem. This self-doubt grew with each encounter, feeding into the confusion and uncertainty that are at the core of gaslighting.

Confrontation as a Battleground

Confrontations become battlegrounds when your words are twisted and used against you. You bring up a genuine concern, but it turns into an argument, leaving you defending your motives rather than addressing the problem. "You always have to make things difficult, don't you?" they accuse, and you find yourself apologizing for having feelings, for simply existing.

Another vivid memory comes to mind—being subtly provoked into a reaction, only to be labeled the villain for reacting. "See how you overreact? This is why we can't have a simple, rational conversation." Any attempt to explain my point of view was met with sheer dismissal

Amidst this chaos, the heart yearns for peace, clinging to fleeting moments of happiness and hope. You recall the joyful times, the shared dreams, and wish for more of those moments. "There must be something worth fighting for," you tell yourself, trying to salvage what you thought was love. But with each cycle, the moments of light grow shorter, replaced by the darkness of doubt and manipulation. The effort to see only the positive becomes a painful reinforcement of a love that once was, now lost in the sands of changed perception.

The Cost of Constant Defense

No one should enter a relationship armed with shields and wearing armor, yet with gaslighting, every conversation feels like a battle. The constant need to justify your feelings, actions, and existence is exhausting, leaving scars on your soul—invisible yet hauntingly painful.

"Why am I always defending myself?" becomes a frequent internal refrain, signaling a deepening crisis of identity and self-worth. It's a fight not just for spoken words and actions, but for your very identity—the last piece of sanity clung to amidst rising waters of self-doubt and mind games.

The Path to Recovery

Recovery begins with awareness—that fleeting moment when you realize you're being manipulated. It's about reclaiming your reality, validating your memories, and trusting your feelings again. This process involves drawing boundaries, reaching out to friends or professionals, and, most crucially, learning to trust yourself once more.

Healing is not linear. It winds through the darkest moments, navigates doubts and setbacks, but each step forward is a step out of the darkness. It's about regaining the personal identity lost to manipulation, finding solidity in your thoughts and feelings, and rediscovering self-love overshadowed by another's need to control.

Why This Matters?

Understanding gaslighting in relationships is crucial for those experiencing it and for anyone seeking healthy, non-toxic love that builds rather than breaks. Remember this: love is wonderful, enriching, and sometimes worth fighting for, but it is never worth losing yourself, your sanity, or your self-esteem. If they didn't always gaslight you, you wouldn't need to constantly defend your reality. And most importantly, it's not your fault. The road to recovery is ahead, leading you back to yourself.

if they didn't... you wouldn't...

REFLECTION OF YOUR SOUL
This is your chance to pour out your feelings and move on.

Tear here. Crumple it up, throw it away and move on.

2

IF THEY DIDN'T ALWAYS DOUBT YOU

2

IF THEY DIDN'T ALWAYS DOUBT YOU

Doubt—when it becomes a constant companion in a relationship—signals the slow erosion of friendship and trust. It starts with small, seemingly innocent doubts but can quickly spiral into a cyclone, tearing apart the bonds that hold two people together. Being constantly questioned about your actions, intentions, and loyalty acts like a slow poison, sapping the joy from your relationship and replacing it with a constant need to defend yourself.

The Dangerous Nature of Doubt

Doubt begins subtly, often disguised as concern or curiosity. Your partner might question why you spent so much time with a friend or why you were late coming home. These inquiries, though minor at first, grow in frequency and intensity. Each question plants a seed of suspicion, which over time, grows into a common sense of distrust. This slow but steady erosion of trust replaces the warmth and genuine connection that should define a loving relationship with a defensive stance. Instead of sharing moments and enjoying each other's company, you find yourself constantly justifying your actions and intentions.

Drawing from personal experiences, I recall when trust was first damaged in a relationship. Positive memories spent with friends were overshadowed by baseless accusations. One particular memory stands out: a casual meeting with friends was perceived as an act of cheating. Though my intentions were honest, and I take no ill will in my heart, the allegation hung over me like a dark cloud that refused to clear, and only shadow of doubt and it left a stain on my heart, a reminder of the pain that doubt can inflict.

In another relationship, I poured my heart into the belief that my love and effort would eventually be recognized and reciprocated. However, every act of affection was scrutinized and often disregarded. The recurring accusation, "You don't love me as much as I love you," became a common refrain, overshadowing my attempts to build a better relationship. What began as acts of love turned into sources of further doubt and frustration. Moments of closeness were tainted by a growing sense of failure and suffering.

The Constant Need to Prove Yourself

Caught in a state of constant self-doubt, you embark on a tiring process of proving your loyalty and love. Relationships become toxic as every action and word are scrutinized, not only by your partner but by yourself as well. You modify your behavior, hold back your true feelings, and smother your partner with affection in a desperate attempt to dispel the doubts that have taken root in their mind.

This continuous strain chips away at your confidence. The doubt cultivated by your partner also alters your self-perception, making you see yourself through the lens of suspicion. You begin to question your worth and the authenticity of your feelings. The pressure to constantly seek approval is exhausting and alters how you view yourself and your place in the relationship.

The Emotional Toll

The emotional toll of unrelenting doubt is immense. It transforms love from a safe haven into a minefield, where every step could trigger a confrontation. The constant need to defend yourself against false claims doesn't bring partners closer; instead, it isolates them, negating the very essence of partnership. Instead of creating memories and happy moments, individuals in such relationships focus on building defenses against the next wave of doubts. The closeness that once existed turns into a warzone, with each partner becoming a litigant in an emotional courtroom. The price paid is immeasurable and deeply felt.

Breaking the Chains of Doubt

Coming out of constant uncertainty is a difficult process of rebuilding one's confidence in one's abilities, and in assessing what constitutes a constructive partnership. It means, deciding how trustful and open you are willing to be with each other, and is based on a quite substantial amount of reflection about what one deserves in terms of relationships.

It is all about how one can demand what he or she wants or needs irrespective of the negative statements by the partner. And perhaps, when all the affection fades away, it's important to understand that love should not be a trial, and affection should not require evidence. Reconstructing trust involves claiming back your own truths, understanding your worth and deciding that one has the right to partner with the heart's desire instead of living in constant insecurity.

Why This Matters?

If you have ever felt 'less than' due to a partner's constant doubting of you, this is a reminder to pay attention to the signs of a relationship that lacks love and is instead filled with suspicion. It's important to become aware of how damaging such toxic interactions can be on a person's sense of self and mental well-being.

Again, if they were not always in doubt, you wouldn't always need to convince them. But there is an opportunity to escape such tendencies and choose a partner whose love can be healthy and nurturing instead of destructive.

if they didn't... you wouldn't...

REFLECTION OF YOUR SOUL
This is your chance to pour out your feelings and move on.

Tear here. Crumple it up, throw it away and move on.

3

IF THEY DIDN'T PRETEND TO LOVE YOU

3

IF THEY DIDN'T PRETEND TO LOVE YOU

Love, when it is pure, does not deceive, scorn, or betray. It is a safe haven of genuine feelings and realism. It is the kind of relationship that fosters a world between two people—a world filled with confidences, laughter, and understanding. But what happens when the anchor you believed in is nothing but an illusion?

The Puzzle of Mixed Signals

So, to grasp the essence of this story—where mixed signals and intertwined fates of people bound by dreams of love led to unexpected outcome, here is a glimpse of my story.

It's a tale of love and bond with deep emotional threads shared between two souls, though with the undertones of doubts and question marks. We dated seven years ago, and after parting ways, life brought us back together. Our reconnection wasn't just old flames that rekindle once again; instead, it was a companionship to survive through the turmoil of life, betrayal through other relationships and we even jokes about getting married to each other if all else failed in our romantic lives. To eyes of those observing our union, we were the epitome of a couple deeply in love.

He was the absolute love of my life, and despite the years and other relationships, my feelings for him never changed. As far as I cared and wanted, that sentiment remained the same until the very last day. He was always on the same page with me, often saying things like, "I know we are the only ones who truly understand how the other feels and who will always stand beside each other." His actions were adoring, loving, intimate, and possessive, making me feel helpless when he pulled me in closer.

But then comes the sting of reality...

There was another side to him that came to light due to the intimacy of our relationship. Despite the love he professed and the intimacy we shared, his eyes wandered, and his heart seemed to wander with them. He was open with me about his interactions with other women, a fact that should have been a clear signal to me and no longer could we say that he truly loved me. Yet, wrapped in the warmth of his nearness, those signals faded into the background until they violently emerged.

The sting came sharply, each time I learned of his flirtations, each time I heard of him fooling around with other women, each time I watched him recreate our intimate moments with someone else. How could the person who felt so perfectly in sync with me, who appeared to understand me in such a profound way, also be pursuing these connections with others on the side? To me, the difference created a conflict that was easy to realize but took time to process. It left a lingering question: as if all that had concerned and touched me was nothing but an illusion?

The Maze of Mixed Emotions

Navigating this maze was challenging. High levels of contact and communication mixed with distancing behaviors and neglect left me feeling crushed. It's one thing to deal with a breakup or straightforward rejection. It's entirely different to question how much someone may or may not like you while they simultaneously ignore your calls and claim to be your friend.

This emotional tug-of-war was not just an issue of jealousy or the feeling that one had been replaced by a younger, more attractive, and better-skilled partner. It was about feeling deceived at my core. It was about the realization that the emotional investments I made were perhaps never matched, that the future we envisioned might never have been seen in the same light by him.

The Quest for Emotional Clarity

The road towards achieving resolution in such cases is long, complicated and requires honest acceptance of certain unpleasant facts. It calls for destroying the images we choose to have or wish we have of a certain person from the actions we choose to bestow on them. If the couple is to move toward resolving issues and healing the relationship, then it involves facing the likelihood that what was believed to be a foundation of love was all based on quicksand.

In this process, the most important thing which is that how one is to differentiate between love and lust. It is about knowing the fact and accepting that the so-called love does not sway with feasibility or availability. The love that one carries for another person should not be mixed with any other kind of love and should not be hidden at any point.

Why This Story Matters?

It is a call to all, who need it, those who struggle with uncertain feelings towards somebody. It has been described as the map toward the dreadful moment when one person does not love another as much as the latter loves him or her, or not in the manner that has been anticipated. May we hate enough to face this reality and begin to demand more for ourselves, to find a love that affirms us, that does not make us question why we are worthy of being in someone's life.

If he didn't give me the sense he loved me, I wouldn't feel so betrayed when I saw him with someone else. This realization isn't just about moving on from him; it is about positioning the readers towards a different concept of love is clear, reciprocal, and worthy of the heart it claims to hold.

if they didn't... you wouldn't...

REFLECTION OF YOUR SOUL
This is your chance to pour out your feelings and move on.

Tear here. Crumple it up, throw it away and move on.

4

IF THEY DIDN'T MAKE YOU WAIT

4

IF THEY DIDN'T MAKE YOU WAIT

In relationships, waiting is often regarded as a positive value—a sign of patience and devotion. But what happens when this waiting becomes a pattern, a one-sided expectation where you are always the one left holding onto hope while the other is absent? This chapter explores the pain of feeling like a backup plan and the journey towards realizing one's own worth.

Always on Call

Consider the life of someone who, despite having their own troubles, is always ready to drop everything for another. This willingness to be available is a virtue admired by many, but it can lead to social inconveniences when it results in unbalanced relationships if the other person does not reciprocate. Sometimes he needed money for an emergency or a friend for company, and there she was, always willing and ready to help, expecting nothing in return. Her life, her time, seemed to orbit around his needs, as if her sole purpose was to be there whenever he called.

This was me—always available, always willing, giving endlessly in the hope that the scales of affection and attention might someday balance out. But instead, what

I received was the pain of canceled plans—a constant reminder that I was never his priority.

The Pain of Canceled Plans

I vividly recall the excitement of planning to meet up with a mutual friend we both considered a sister. But often, we were sometimes let down by requests we made, and I always found myself at the mercy of his whims and availabilities. Whenever I initiated the plan, he would frequently come up with last-minute excuses about being stuck, which put me in an uncomfortable and awkward position, making me appear unreliable to others. Conversely, whenever he proposed an outing, there was an expectation that we must attend, whether I wanted to or not. There was a clear imbalance—he had the privilege of defining and dictating his needs and commitments, whereas mine were easily dismissed.

This isn't just about missing one event—it's about the repeated crushing of enthusiasm, the slow realization that my needs and desires are always secondary and this pattern of last-minute cancellation besides being frustrating, was also a clear signal regarding standing last in his list of priorities.

Silence When It Suits Him

There's also the stinging silence when he just says he's busy with many things or pretends to have a lot of work to do. Of course, being busy is a valid part of life, but a simple message, even in the busiest times, takes just a minute and is enough to show care. Yet, such courtesies were missing, and I was always left stranded with the feeling of being neglected in the relationship. This paints a clear picture—'She is there for him, but he is not there for her, at least not in the ways that truly matter.'

I always valued him, perhaps more than I valued myself, placing his needs and happiness above my own. However, such a relationship always leads to dissatisfaction and the feeling of inadequacy, which only intensifies the feelings of low self-worth. The journey to recognizing one's worth begins with understanding that being caring and supportive should not entail losing oneself in the process. It is about defining relationship bounds and turning it into a partnership where respect is both given and expected.

Recognizing Your Worth

Realizing that if someone continually makes you wait, continually sees you as an option rather than a priority, then perhaps it's time to reassess not just the relationship but also how you value yourself. This recognition is crucial for those who have ever been left waiting, feeling like a backup plan. It's a call to understand the signs of being treated as secondary and to realize that everyone deserves to feel valued and prioritized by their loved ones.

The Emotional Toll

The emotional toll of being made to wait, of being seen as less important, is profound. It eats away at your self-esteem and makes you question your worth. You start to wonder if you are truly deserving of love and attention, or if your role is to always be the one waiting in the wings. This kind of emotional erosion can have long-lasting effects, making it difficult to trust and engage fully in future relationships.

Breaking Free from the Waiting Game

Breaking free from the cycle of waiting and being undervalued requires strength and self-awareness. It involves recognizing your own worth and understanding that you deserve a partner who respects and values your time and emotions. It's about setting boundaries and not being afraid to demand the respect and attention you deserve.

Waiting can be a virtue in relationships, but when it becomes a one-sided expectation, it can lead to feelings of inadequacy and low self-worth. Recognizing the signs of being treated as a backup plan and taking steps to reclaim your self-worth is crucial for your emotional well-being. If someone continually makes you wait, it's time to reassess the relationship and ensure that your feelings are valued and respected. You deserve to be in a relationship where you are a priority, not an option.

if they didn't... you wouldn't...

REFLECTION OF YOUR SOUL
This is your chance to pour out your feelings and move on.

Tear here. Crumple it up, throw it away and move on.

5

IF THEY DIDN'T CLAIM YOU WERE A PRIORITY

5

IF THEY DIDN'T CLAIM YOU WERE A PRIORITY

In relationships, the promise of being someone's priority is held like a beacon; it's a declaration that amidst the chaos of life, there's someone who will choose you first. However, when this promise is broken repeatedly, it chips away at the very foundation of trust and mutual respect.

The Illusion of Priority

Envision a relationship where you consistently place someone else's needs above your own, regardless of your own struggles or challenges. This was the essence of my commitment to him. The reason might have been a financial crisis or the occasional longing for someone to talk to, I was always there. Still, there seemed to be an unwritten understanding that this level of involvement would be met with a similar level of commitment in return and that the ratio of who has given more and who has given less would not be tilted for eternity. However, the reality often told a starkly different story.

A Broken Promise

Take, for instance, the time when we were meant to meet

someone who meant the world to me—my best friend who has been by my side through thick and thin. She was celebrating something very important to her, and he promised he would be there. I had been counting down the days, excited to introduce her to him and bring together parts of my life that had been split into two completely different worlds. Despite his continuous reassurances and promises, his last-minute absence stung with disappointment and betrayal. The excitement that had built up inside me, imagining the laughter and stories we would share together, collapsed.

His avoidance of this meaningful meeting, especially at the time when he was aware of my feelings, did not only reveal a lot about him but it was insulting too. It was like as if my worth was dismissed, and even of those aspects I hold most dear. It felt like his flowery words about the importance of our relationship meant nothing.

The Weight of Silence

Even in our everyday interactions, his lack of communication spoke volumes. Each day he didn't bother to respond—not even a simple text or call to acknowledge my existence—made me feel increasingly unimportant. His frequent claims of being too busy were contradicted by his silence. In relationships, maintaining open lines of communication, even brief check-ins, is fundamental. His so-called busy schedules and numerous excuses for not attending to my needs clearly indicated that I was becoming unimportant to him.

Because Silence Speaks Volume... and his so-called busy schedules and the numerous excuses he gave me for not attending to my needs were a clear indication that I was becoming unimportant to him as a girlfriend.

Also, his consistent failure to do even these bare minimum planted seeds of doubt and underscored my role as an afterthought rather than a priority which not only made me question my relationship with my boyfriend but also brought the disparity of our feelings to me.

The Imbalance of Emotional Investment

The difference in how much one values someone versus how they are valued in return can lead to profound feelings of inadequacy and neglect. For someone who consistently places others above themselves, like I did, it becomes a harsh lesson in self-worth. The realization that you are not as important to someone as they are to you can be both eye-opening and heart-wrenching.

Recognizing and Reclaiming Your Worth

Coming to terms with not being someone's priority, despite their assurances, is a painful realization. It forces a reevaluation of one's own worth and the dynamics of the relationship. This redemption calls for taking a stand and discovering how to put oneself first. It is about the understanding that one can be a giver and compassionate, and at the same time, avoid invasive self-sacrifice.

The repeated cycle of disappointment, being let down time to time—from planning activities together to him backing off at the last moment is tiresome, drains emotional energy and detracts from the trust built in the relationship.

The reality often painted a different story from the promises made. Sometimes it revealed a picture that was quite a far cry from the beautiful picture being drawn. The continuous cycle of being told I was everything to him—his "everything" in words but not in deeds was an unbroken loop of being assured that he needed me more than anything in this world, but his actions were a completely different story. Such a constant flip-flopping between words and deeds created a toxic cycle of doubt and confusion.

Setting Boundaries for Self-Preservation

Accepting these harsh truths forces coming to terms with these realities prompts a painful but necessary reevaluation of one's worth and the dynamics of the relationship. It's about realizing that being supportive and caring do not entail constantly putting other's needs before our own. Setting boundaries is crucial, not just for personal well-being but also for preserving the integrity of what a relationship should represent—a mutual exchange of respect and affection, not a one-sided affair.

One has to set boundaries in order to avoid being used and to lock up a simple virtue that a relationship is not some sort of a business deal where one party is being exploited but rather, relationships should be a beautiful thing where people share respect for one another and affection and not just a one-sided affair.

This chapter is a call to action for those who find themselves always waiting, always hoping, and consistently disappointed. It's about learning to not just forgive but also to demand a reciprocal level of commitment and respect. If they didn't make you wait or claim you were a priority without meaning it, you wouldn't have to endure the recurring pain of feeling undervalued.

Remember, Understanding Your Worth Matters!

It is crucial to comprehend it as a first step toward a healthy relationship which impels a person to be a priority for someone. If they didn't claim you were a priority, you wouldn't have to face the recurring pain of realizing you are not. But through these experiences, there is an opportunity for growth—to learn that your worth is not defined by how much you sacrifice for others, but by recognizing and insisting upon the respect and love you truly deserve.

This narrative isn't just about recognizing the signs of being sidelined; it's about insisting on—and receiving—the love, respect, and priority you rightfully deserve. It's about not letting anyone dim the light of your self-worth with the shadows of their inconsistency.

This chapter encourages a redefinition of what it means

to be a priority in someone's life and prompts a reflection on ensuring that actions align with words, ensuring that promises made are promises kept. Remember, a relationship is about balance, give and take, not just take. If they truly see you as their priority, their actions will speak as loudly as their words.

if they didn't... you wouldn't...

REFLECTION OF YOUR SOUL
This is your chance to pour out your feelings and move on.

Tear here. Crumple it up, throw it away and move on.

6

IF THEY DIDN'T HIDE THEIR FEELINGS

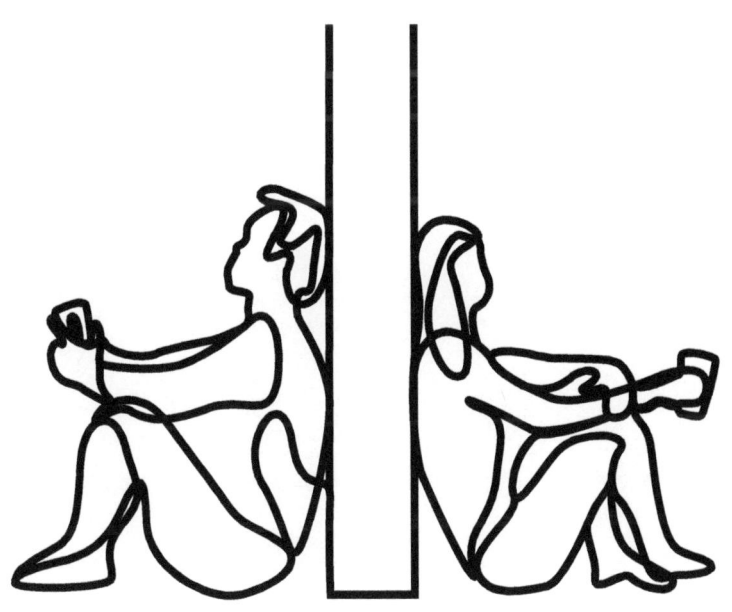

6

IF THEY DIDN'T HIDE THEIR FEELINGS

Communication is indeed the lifeline of any relationship, serving as the essential channel through which partners can truly connect, resolve conflicts, and share their deepest feelings. But what happens when one partner consistently hides their emotions?

When this communication breakdown happens, especially when one partner withdraws their affection, the consequences are severe, which is not only a breakdown of the relationship's healthy state but also partners' mental health. This chapter delves into the confusion and guilt that arise when one person in the relationship is unable to openly express what they feel but, first let's understand '**The Importance of Sharing Feelings**'

Sharing feelings in a relationship is crucial because it fosters trust and deepens intimacy. When partners openly express their emotions, they allow their partners to peek into their souls. In fact, that vulnerability is the basis for building intimacy and empathy between the two partners. It reassures both partners that they are in a safe space where they can be honest and open without fear of judgment, or being confined or punished.

The Effects of Withheld Emotions

When people fail to express their emotions in words, several problems may occur:

Misunderstandings and Assumptions: Without clear communication, partners may misinterpret each other's actions or moods. When expectations aren't communicated, assumptions are often made, which can fuel conflicts and misunderstandings that could have been easily avoided with open dialogue.

Emotional Distance: Consistently hiding emotions and being quiet all the time affects the displays of affection, which in turn leads to the construction of emotional walls. As time passes, such distancing can lead to a decrease in the level of affection in the relationship, with partners simply becoming roommates rather than a passionate and loving couple.

Resentment and Frustration: While the partner on the receiving end of such emotionally charged silence may feel they are being reminded of the fact that the other person does not value or care for them anymore, and this often breeds resentment. This resentment may remain hidden and accumulate over time and may reach a boiling point where the couples quarrel or have conflicts over issues arising from such unmet needs.

Stress and Anxiety: As for the individual who battles silently with his or her emotions, it will subject himself/herself to more stress and anxiety due to suppressed feelings. Holding back emotions requires constant self-monitoring and energy, which can be exhausting and damaging to one's mental health.

To address these challenges, couples must ensure that they maintain the spirit of truthfulness in the relationships. This involves:

- Counseling once in a while about how each partner feels and the things that happen during the day also allows for positive emotions to be shared.
- If one is speaking, the other should listen in a non-judgmental manner, meaning the listener puts great effort in paying attention to all that is being uttered minus the fuss of the response that one is about to give. This causes the speaker to feel valued and acknowledged by their counterpart.
- Being encouraging when one wants to tell something to the other about his or her feelings and being genuinely supportive when they do, goes a long way in strengthening the sense of safety between partners.
- The belief that one can handle the other's response to their emotions likely encourages partners to share more often. For example, reacting with anger or dismissal can discourage openness, while a calm, supportive response can foster it.I

The Enigma of Unspoken Emotions

I experienced firsthand the confusion of a relationship where discussions about feelings and future plans were met with vague responses or complete avoidance. He often mentioned that due to past issues, he found it difficult to convey his emotions or envision a future together. His assurances were always general: "We will always be there for each other, no matter what." But beyond this, there was a void—no definite decisions, no goals, no clear vision of the direction in which our relationship was heading.

This lack of clarity was not limited to a personal aspect it spilled over into our social circles and complicates our interactions with others around us. Whenever friends asked me about what our relationship is, he would always give inconclusive responses that kept everyone including myself confused. This was so frustrating—so lonely, as it put me in the awkward position of having to explain or justify our dynamic to others without truly understanding it myself and without necessarily knowing why we were like this.

Why is it that he could be so affectionate in public, so seemingly committed in the eyes of others, yet so detached in private? This variance was puzzling. He was eager to put on the show that he was a loving and caring boyfriend whenever we were with others while failing to show the same passion whenever we were alone. It felt as if our relationship was more about fake appearances merely on public exchange than genuine connection.

He only demonstrated his further affection when I was most fragile, and in many cases when I was facing a personal difficulty, assuring me of his support and care. But why did it take such extreme circumstances for him to open up? This pattern made it difficult to gauge where it was hard to tell whether the feelings expressed were genuine or they were a result of pressure due to the situation.

The Rollercoaster of Arguments

Now that the intensity of our quarrels was included towards the equation, the emotional aspect of the relationship was already complicated enough. In the heat of disagreement, he would suggest that perhaps we were not meant to be together. Yet, it was often after these conflicts, when tensions had peaked, that he would declare his love and insist on how much I meant to him. This cycle of conflict and reconciliation was very tiring with a break almost repeats every morning to the night, which raises question that 'Why did it take some arguments and threat of separation for people to start professing their love to each other?'

This chapter thus paints a clear picture of how it is necessary to be truthful and open to feelings in each relationship. It examines the effect of the lack of affection that a feeble person has on the targets, or how the targets are confused when they are shown mixed signals and occasional affection by their partners.

Recoginizing the Value of Communication

For a relationship to achieve psychological well-being and stability, both partners must appreciate the value of communication. If he hadn't hidden his emotions, our relationship wouldn't have been reduced to mere exchanges of greetings, kisses, or touches. Instead, it could have led to a much stronger bond.

To everyone who struggles with similar scenarios, this chapter serves as a reminder that everyone deserves a partner who is present with their emotions during the highs and lows, and also in the quiet moments when reassurance is needed. It encourages readers to choose open-hearted communication in relationships, which fosters strength and creates a foundation based on trust and deep understanding.

if they didn't... you wouldn't...

REFLECTION OF YOUR SOUL
This is your chance to pour out your feelings and move on.

Tear here. Crumple it up, throw it away and move on.

7

IF THEY DIDN'T BREAK PROMISES

7

IF THEY DIDN'T BREAK PROMISES

Promises are the threads that weave the fabric of trust in a relationship. They are affirmations of commitment, are the stitches that hold the quilt of confidence in a relationship. They are expressions of loyalty and assurance signaling to the other with small contracts that say, "You can count on me," "You are safe and can rely on me." But what happens when these promises are repeatedly broken? What about when these assurances are repeatedly violated? This chapter explores the emotional toll of forgiving broken promises time and again, and the critical importance of setting boundaries repeatedly as well as the role of boundary setting to protect one's emotional well-being.

The Cycle of Excitement and Disappointment

Imagine the simple joy of planning to attend a concert with someone, especially when it involves a singer both of you adore. The initial promise is made with shared excitement, kindling a spark of joyful anticipation. However, this spark is abruptly snuffed out when, just days later, he dismisses the plan as "not worth it." It is not just frustrating but also energy-consuming to have one's hopes raised, only to be crushed a minute later.

Each broken promise might seem minor in isolation—a concert here, a missed drinking date there—but collectively, they form a pattern that erodes trust. It is not simply hopeless here but generates further feelings of insecurity because of disbelief that reaches far beyond the simple frustration. When promises are not kept, the message is clear: Such realization sounds like, "You cannot rely on me." It really takes a toll on you especially when in spoken words, he reminds you constantly of how important you are to him. By his words, yet always he behaves in the opposite way to mean it, thus causing one a dilemma to confront.

This puts you always in a state of wait, which never arrives because the things that are being promised is always different from what is being delivered. You cannot know whether to take the words at face value or to prepare for the opposite of what is being said. This uncertainty is one of the most toxic aspects of this dynamic because it can paralyze, impacting not only the relationship, but also your self-worth and ability to make decisions in other aspects of your life. The question looms large: If he cannot do simple things as he promised, how much more when it comes to larger commitments?

The Silent Erosion of Trust

Each broken promise chips away at the foundation of the relationship, creating cracks of doubt and resentment. Trust is built on the consistency of words and actions. When promises are broken, it signals a lack of respect and consideration for the other person's feelings and time. This silent erosion of trust can be more damaging than outright betrayal because it is insidious, slowly undermining the relationship's integrity.

I recall an instance where he promised to be there for an important event, a moment that held significant emotional value for me. The anticipation of his support and presence gave me strength. But as the day approached, his excuses began to pile up—work commitments, unexpected errands, and finally, silence. The absence of his presence at that crucial moment was not just a broken promise; it was a stark reminder of how little my needs and emotions mattered in the grand scheme of his life.

The Toll of Broken Promises

The emotional toll of forgiving broken promises repeatedly is profound. It creates a cycle of hope and disappointment, leaving you emotionally exhausted and vulnerable. You start to question your worth and whether you deserve to be treated with respect and consideration. This constant questioning can lead to a diminished sense of self-worth and a pervasive feeling of insecurity.

It is important to recognize that forgiveness does not mean accepting repeated disrespect. Forgiving someone does not absolve them of the responsibility to change their behavior. True forgiveness involves setting boundaries to protect yourself from any further harm. It means understanding that while you can forgive, you must also hold the other person accountable for all of their actions.

Setting Boundaries to Protect Yourself

Learning to draw lines every time someone has a habit of making a lot of promises but rarely delivers is crucial. Boundaries are not just lines drawn with the intention of preventing people from getting close; they also set a certain standard for the other person. These boundaries send a clear message that forgiveness is available in the relationship, but it is not to be exploited as a license to continue making the same mistakes.

Indeed, forgiveness is a vital and constructive element that shall be rendered in any kind of relationship. However, there is a thin line that separates forgiveness from putting up excuses for people. Sometimes when forgiveness is given for this and that because of broken promises, the entire process is made to be routine so that such individuals are free to continue disrespecting. It is important that one should understand this difference in order to preserve one's dignity as well as one's emotional well-being.

Setting boundaries means communicating your needs and expectations clearly. It means saying, "I value you and this relationship, but I also value myself. If you continue to break promises, it tells me that you do not value me or my time." Boundaries are about respecting yourself enough to demand the respect you deserve from others.

The Thin Line Between Forgiveness and Enabling

Indeed, forgiveness is a vital and constructive element in any kind of relationship. However, there is a thin line that separates forgiveness from putting up excuses for people. Sometimes when forgiveness is provided repeatedly for broken promises, it becomes a routine, enabling individuals to continue disrespecting you. It is important to understand this difference to preserve your dignity and emotional well-being.

Forgiveness should be accompanied by a call for change. It should be a moment of reflection for both parties, an opportunity to address the behavior that led to the broken promise and to work towards a solution. If the behavior continues, it is a sign that the other person is not willing to change, and it might be time to reconsider the relationship.

Moving Forward with Clarity

This chapter is a good reminder that trust is the essential ingredient in love, but it is also critical to work on sustaining that trust as the day-to-day reality happens. It challenges readers to think about their own personal relationships and to look for patterns of infidelity and unfaithfulness, motivating them to protect themselves and set up barriers that will prevent further betrayal.

If he did not fail in promises, the relations map would look very differently." There would be far more stability and trust in relationships. Nevertheless, there would be no sense in complaining that this is not the situation at the present time, if people do not want a change. Whether it's sitting down to discuss how one's actions have affected both of you, or considering whether the relationship is healthy for both parties, it's about progressing toward a point where your feelings are not only acknowledged but also understood.

Reclaiming Your Self-Worth

In essence, this chapter is a wake-up call for anyone who has felt the pressure of broken promises to not only look for but also demand more so that a heart that was freely given does not feel the pinch of poor handling. It is about reclaiming your self-worth and understanding that you deserve a relationship built on mutual respect and trust.

if they didn't... you wouldn't...

REFLECTION OF YOUR SOUL
This is your chance to pour out your feelings and move on.

Tear here. Crumple it up. throw it away and move on.

8

IF THEY DIDN'T FEEL LIKE YOUR FOREVER PERSON

8

IF THEY DIDN'T FEEL LIKE YOUR FOREVER PERSON

In the plot of our lives, the feeling of destiny, especially in matters concerning the heart, is something that we cannot easily let go of. Believing that someone is your soulmate and that you'll be together forever can be both a blessing and a curse. This chapter reflects on the difficult process of understanding when love turns from an anchor to a chain, and the liberating realization that to find a real 'happily ever after,' one must sometimes let go.

The Myth of the Forever Person

Imagine believing so deeply in the connection with someone that every path leads back to them, regardless of the circumstances. This was my reality with him—no matter how many times our world turned upside down, we always ended up coming back to one another. We had this understanding that it was destined to be between us, and we had always been each other's cushion, packaged with our shared history. We believed anything could be solved because we had always been there for each other.

However, it has disguised the basic realities of our relationship where things were not as inevitable as they seemed. Although it was somewhat meant to be, it pretty much prevented personal development and logically, the search for potentially more fulfilling relationships. His companionship was both highly comforting and highly confining because having him by my side offered me a sense of security and stability, while also not allowing me to explore horizons and live a life that was different from the one we had together.

There was no doubt that the special comfort given to each other could not be gained in any other way. It was a stable ground from the uncertainties of the world, a familiar place where we could fully express ourselves. Yet, this very comfort posed a crucial question: Were we clinging to each other because of the affection we had for the other, or had grown used to having that specific person around? The tendencies to repeat the same patterns clearly overshadowed the efforts required to build new relationships, as well as to develop separately.

In each new potential relationship, it was impossible not to measure them by the worth of our previous experience. How would he feel? How would this new person compare to someone who knew my former life and how long I had been struggling? It's not only that such comparisons we are unable to draw were unjust, but they were also incapable of being made at all. It made me constantly connect me to the material world and to my past, thus denying me the opportunity to embrace the future.

The Fear of Moving On

The thought of truly moving on brought a mix of fear

and guilt. Fear of the unknown—could someone else truly understand me as he did? Regret for the fact that the story that we constructed, that we were two people who are made for each other, might be destroyed. These emotional rollercoasters were further compounded by the cultural beliefs and pressure from the society which perceived us as theoretically perfect partners meant to be together.

Moving on felt like betraying a dream we had both built and cherished. The fear of starting over, of finding someone new, and the possibility of never finding a connection as deep and meaningful was paralyzing. It felt safer to stay within the confines of our familiar yet unfulfilling relationship than to venture into the unknown.

Finding the Courage to Seek Happiness

It was time for a change, the change which would lead me on the journey of finding my own happily ever after. It called for understanding that it is impossible for one's happiness to depend on another person's feelings, despite the fact that people share such elements of existence as life, love, and work. And then, I meant being able to accept him as part of my story but not the core or center of it. I learned to appreciate him as a chapter in my life's story but not the entire book.

Letting go of the idea that he was my forever person was not a betrayal of our past but an affirmation of my self-worth and future. It was a great motivation to go out and find an individual who could provide warmth and also help me evolve in a new direction. This process was not about searching for someone flawless; it was about searching for someone who would be right for the person I was gradually becoming.

Finding the courage to seek happiness meant embracing the possibility of multiple happily ever afters. It meant understanding that love is not a singular, unchanging entity but a dynamic and evolving force that can manifest in various forms and through different people.

Your Happily Ever After is Out There

If they weren't your forever person, it doesn't spell the end of love—it marks the beginning of a new journey towards self-discovery and fulfillment. This chapter is a call to those feeling stuck in the orbit of a past relationship to venture out and explore, to believe in the possibility of multiple happily ever afters, and to find the courage to pursue them.

I hope that this chapter will speak to anyone who has ever felt that they are living in a world dictated by past events and finding ways to begin anew with hope and purpose. It is a concept that, in my opinion, can be best translated as learning to accept and realize that sometimes, the greatest way to give back to a special friendship is to acknowledge the fact that all good things come to an end, and, the best way to honor the bond that one had for the other is by moving on, leaving a spot in one's heart to be filled with new stories and adventures to be written,

if they didn't... you wouldn't...

REFLECTION OF YOUR SOUL
This is your chance to pour out your feelings and move on.

Tear here. Crumple it up, throw it away and move on.

9

IF THEY DIDN'T CREATE THE WOUNDS

9

IF THEY DIDN'T CREATE THE WOUNDS

The Path to Healing Begins

Hope of trying to define how to recover from emotional pain was a better one, but again it's a process and every person is different. Healing from emotional wounds is not a straightforward journey. It's a complex, multifaceted process that varies from person to person. It starts when one concentrates on the attempts to repair the cracks created by repeated disappointments and failures. This chapter outlines the crucial first steps toward healing: acknowledging the pain, accepting the need for change, and beginning the process of emotional remedy.

Acknowledging the Pain

The journey to healing begins with the simple, yet profound act of acknowledging that you are hurt. This step involves giving yourself permission to feel disappointment, sadness, or anger, and admitting that things did not turn out as you had hoped. This admission is not a sign of weakness; rather, it is a mark of strength and self-awareness. It requires courage to face the reality of your emotions and to allow yourself to grieve the loss of what might have been.

Acknowledging pain also means facing uncomfortable truths about the situation and yourself. It involves recognizing the impact of past events on your current emotional state. It's about understanding that feeling hurt is a natural response to unmet expectations and that these emotions are valid and worthy of attention. Allowing yourself to experience these feelings is an essential step toward healing and recovery.

Learning from Disappointment

Every disappointment carries valuable lessons. It's crucial to extract these lessons to avoid repeating the same mistakes in the future. Disappointments, though painful, are opportunities for growth and self-improvement. Reflecting can help you identify patterns and recurring situations that cause you pain. This self-awareness is key to developing healthier coping mechanisms and making better choices in future relationships.

While it may seem that disappointment is an inevitable part of life, understanding its causes and learning from them can help mitigate its effects. This might involve setting clearer boundaries, recognizing red flags earlier, or gaining a better perspective on yourself and your needs. Each lesson learned is a step towards emotional well-being and resilience.

Focusing on Self Growth

In consequence of the feeling of pain, focusing on

self-growth can be a powerful way to cope and heal. Engage in activities that contribute positively to your life and bring you joy and fulfillment. Whether it's diving into a passion project, spending quality time with friends and family, or revisiting a favorite hobby, these activities can provide solace and a sense of normalcy amidst chaos.

Self-growth also involves nurturing your well-being through self-care practices. Prioritize your physical and mental health by engaging in activities that promote relaxation and happiness. This might include exercise, mindfulness practices, or pursuing new interests that invigorate your spirit. The goal is to create a sense of balance and contentment in your life, independent of past wounds.

During tough times, the support of friends and family becomes invaluable. They act as pillars of strength, providing comfort and encouragement when you feel too weak to stand alone. Don't hesitate to lean on these relationships for support. Sharing your struggles with someone who cares can lighten your emotional load and remind you that you are not alone in your journey.

The Gradual Nature of Healing

Remember that healing is a gradual process. There will be good days and bad days, and it's essential to be patient and kind to yourself throughout. Healing is not an instantaneous recovery but a journey of gradual progress. Allow yourself the time and space to heal at your own pace. Embrace the ups and downs, knowing that each step, no matter how small, contributes to your overall well-being.

Embrace the Light Ahead!

Navigating through the dark web of painful memories can be daunting and harrowing, but it is important to recognize that there is always a glimmer of hope at the end of the road. Every small step forward is a movement toward a happier, healthier you. Healing is not about erasing the past but about learning to live with the scars and emerging stronger and more resilient.

It's essential to celebrate each milestone, no matter how minor it may seem. Each day that you wake up bearing the scars but feeling a little less weak, a little less broken, is a victory. Embrace the light ahead with hope and optimism, knowing that you are making progress. Healing is a journey filled with ups and downs, but it is also a path to self-discovery and renewal.

As you move forward, remember that your past does not define your future. You have the power to shape your own story and to create a life filled with love, joy, and fulfillment. Embrace the journey of healing with courage and determination, and trust that you are moving toward a brighter, more hopeful future.

if they didn't... you wouldn't...

REFLECTION OF YOUR SOUL
This is your chance to pour out your feelings and move on.

Tear here. Crumple it up, throw it away and move on.

10

IF THEY DIDN'T LOVE YOU

10

IF THEY DIDN'T LOVE YOU

When we love, we open our hearts fully, trusting that our affection will be reciprocated. In any loving relationship, there's an internal expectation of mutual exchange—of support, understanding, and feelings. Lovers anticipate a partnership where both give and receive, creating a balance that deepens their connection and enhances their mutual respect and admiration.

However, the realization that the affection you give is not returned can be deeply painful. This imbalance, where one's feelings are not met with the same intensity or dedication, can lead to a sense of rejection and loneliness, challenging the very foundations of one's emotional world. However, this chapter explores how such experiences, while challenging, can also be transformative, leading you to a deeper understanding and appreciation of self-love.

The Value of Self-Love

Self-love is the foundation upon which healing from unreturned affection is built. It's about respecting yourself enough to accept that not every relationship will work in your favor and that this is okay.

This kind of self-respect empowers you to accept relationship outcomes that might not always align with your hopes, without internalizing these experiences as personal failures. It teaches you to detach your self-worth from the dynamics of your relationships and to understand that just because someone fails to reciprocate your affection, it does not diminish your importance or desirability based on someone's inability to see it.

Moreover, self-love involves actively caring for and nurturing oneself, especially in the face of emotional pain. It means prioritizing your well-being and happiness, making choices that sustain your mental, emotional, and physical health. When you truly value and love yourself, you set healthy boundaries that prevent others from diminishing your spirit or taking your love for granted.

The Role of Acceptance

Acknowledgment that somebody does not love in a particular manner desired, or does not love at all, is a considerable and normally painful stage in the process of rebuilding. These emotions are, however, important for the development of the individual self and overcoming of the painful experience. It does not mean that the love you felt was an illusion or disappeared; it allows for a new perspective concerning that love as part of the overall life experience.

Acceptance makes it possible to change your perception about unrequited love and see it as one of the many experiences you can undergo in your lifetime. It means understanding that if some people do not reciprocate in one relationship, it does not make you a failure or mean that there is something lacking in you. Rather, it underscores the fact that love is a reciprocal exchange between two lovers and is also influenced by timing. It does not mean that anyone and everyone who finds a connection can make it a lifetime of togetherness.

Generally, accepting this perspective allows one to escape the burden of unfulfilled anticipations. It comes down to the notion that love cannot be forced or forced to stop simply because the other person does not feel the same way. This helps to ensure that you do not develop a disposition that interprets rejection as part of your worth.

Moreover, this acceptance empowers you to continue loving and valuing yourself, maintaining your openness to future relationships without fear. It underscores the importance of not letting one-sided affection close your heart but instead using it as a steppingstone to deeper self-knowledge and emotional resilience.

In sum, accepting unreciprocated love is about understanding that while you can offer your love, you cannot control the response and regardless of its outcome, is a valuable part of your journey—a chapter in your story, but not the entire narrative. This realization ensures that your capacity to give and receive love remains intact and vibrant, ready for a future where love flows both to and from you in equal measure.

Finding Value and Strength in Being Alone

Solitude often carries a negative meaning, but in the context of healing, it can be incredibly powerful as it provides the space to reflect, grow, and fortify yourself. In solitude, you are presented with a unique opportunity to delve deep into your own needs, desires, and feelings without the influence or distraction of others. This allows you to reconnect with who you are at your core, beyond your roles and relationships. It's a chance to ask yourself what truly makes you happy, what you value in life, and how you want to shape your future.

It's a time when you can explore new hobbies, revisit old interests, and perhaps most importantly, cultivate your mental and emotional well-being. You can set your own pace for recovery and growth, listening closely to your inner voice.

Furthermore, solitude provides you with the space to reflect on past relationships from a place of distance and perspective. Without the immediate emotional turmoil that often accompanies breakups or emotional disappointments, you can more objectively assess what went wrong and what you truly need from a partner. This understanding is crucial for entering future relationships with a clearer sense of what will best support your emotional health and happiness.

Learning from the Past

Reflecting on past relationships through the lens of

education and growth rather than regret allows for a more constructive and empowering perspective on personal history. Each relationship, regardless of its duration or ultimate outcome, holds valuable lessons that can inform and enrich your future interactions and personal development.

These interactions teach us about our own behaviors, responses, and emotional triggers, highlighting areas where we may need to grow or adjust. By examining past relationships, we can gain clarity on patterns that may have contributed to challenges or conflicts, such as communication styles, boundaries, or compatibility issues.

In addition to teaching us about dynamics with others, relationships are profound mirrors that reflect our deepest desires, fears, and values. They force us to confront aspects of ourselves that we might otherwise ignore or suppress. For instance, a relationship might reveal a tendency to prioritize others' needs over our own, or it might highlight our resilience in the face of adversity.

It also provides critical insights into human behavior and relationship dynamic and teach us how different personalities interact, what emotional needs look like in various contexts, and how they can be healthily addressed.

Perhaps most importantly, reflecting on past relationships helps clarify the type of love you deserve. It brings into focus what qualities are most important to you in a partner and what relationship dynamics are most conducive to your wellbeing. Armed with this knowledge, you can build a stronger, more aware version of yourself that make you better equipped to handle future relationships and enhances your overall life satisfaction.

The Pillars of Support

While advocating for self-sufficiency, it is also important to understand when it is appropriate to depend on your loved ones. True healing involves both self-reflection and the support of a community. Close friends and family can offer advice and encouragement when you are unable to do so for yourself or when they see you need a push.

Remember, recovering from unreciprocated love does not mean filling the gap with another person. It's about filling that void yourself with love, respect, and acceptance. This chapter is about learning to stand on your own and the beauty of creating a world of happiness without the need for external affection.

if they didn't... you wouldn't...

REFLECTION OF YOUR SOUL
This is your chance to pour out your feelings and move on.

Tear here. Crumple it up, throw it away and move on.

CONCLUSION

CONCLUSION

The process of healing from heartbreak to independence is a deeply personal and profoundly transformative journey. It involves transitioning from a state of distress, anger, and disappointment caused by unrequited love and betrayal to a place of self-acceptance and confidence. This journey ultimately leads to the readiness to seek a partner who reciprocates your feelings and values you for who you are. Words cannot fully convey how much I appreciate your strength and resilience. I encourage you to take back control of your life, to love yourself deeply, and to seek a partner who truly appreciates and adds value to your existence.

Love lost is an experience that many of us endure at some point in our lives. While the pain of such loss can be shocking and profound, it is a universal experience. It may tear at the very fabric of our hope, but it also speaks volumes about our capacity for love and the depth of our emotions. This experience, though painful, serves as a powerful wake-up call, revealing our strengths and weaknesses and prompting us to reflect on our lives and the directions we are heading.

At the core of this transformative journey is the principle of self-love. This concept goes beyond the popular saying and delves into a vital understanding of one's incoherent value and worthiness. Self-love acts as a protective shield and a source of nourishment during the toughest and most desperate moments of our lives. It provides a solid foundation upon which we can stand even when the world around us seems to be collapsing. By dedicating time to love and care for yourself, you create a strong, resilient heart, ready to welcome love again, but this time on your own terms.

In these quiet moments of solitude, you have the opportunity to reflect, to dream anew, and to plan your future without compromise. This personal journey is profoundly empowering, but the role of a supportive community cannot be overstated. Friends, family, and sometimes even strangers become mirrors reflecting our worth back to us when we are unable to see it ourselves. Their support and encouragement are invaluable as we navigate the path to healing and empowerment.

Remember to Turn Your Pain into Power!

Every experience of heartbreak carries the seeds of empowerment. Each setback teaches us more about what we truly need from a relationship and what we are capable of giving. We learn to refine our boundaries and enhance our ability to say 'NO' to what does not serve us and 'YES' to what uplifts us. This process of learning and growth is integral to building a more fulfilling future.

As you move forward, remember that there will be days of doubt and moments of weakness. However, each step forward, no matter how small, is a step towards a brighter, more fulfilling future. Hold onto the lessons learned, cherish the strength gained, and approach each new day with hope and optimism.

> "You may not control all the events that happen to you, but you can decide not to be reduced by them."
> — Maya Angelou

This quote is a powerful reminder of the incredible control we have over our own lives. While we may not choose our circumstances, we have the power to choose our responses. In doing so, we reclaim our power and independence, shaping our lives according to our own values and aspirations.

This conclusion is not merely the end of a book but an invitation to a new beginning in your life. It is a call to those who have felt the sting of heartbreak to embrace their journey of healing and empowerment. Remember, you are the author of your own life story. Write a narrative rich with love—starting with self-love—and vibrant with resilience and hope. With every flipped page, you are inching closer to a life filled with love, joy, and true contentment.

Only You Can Create Your Own Happy Ending! Take the lessons learned from past experiences, harness the strength you have gained, and move forward with confidence and determination. Your journey toward a brighter, more fulfilling future is just beginning. Embrace it with open arms, knowing that you have the power to shape your destiny and create a life that truly reflects your worth and potential.

if they didn't...
you wouldn't...

Christelle Faith Menon

Milton Keynes UK
Ingram Content Group UK Ltd.
UKHW030654090924
448088UK00004B/259